28.01.2001

This book belongs to :-

Karen Baldwin.

CW00953886

STEPHANIE DOWRICK

Daily Acts of Love

VIKING

Penguin Books Australia Ltd
487 Maroondah Highway, PO Box 257
Ringwood, Victoria 3134, Australia
Penguin Books Ltd
Harmondsworth, Middlesex, England
Penguin Putnam Inc.
375 Hudson Street, New York, New York 10014, USA
Penguin Books Canada Limited
10 Alcorn Avenue, Toronto, Ontario, Canada M4V 3B2
Penguin Books (NZ) Ltd
Cnr Rosedale and Airborne Roads, Albany, Auckland, New Zealand
Penguin Books (South Africa) (Pty) Ltd
4 Pallinghurst Road, Parktown 2193, South Africa

First published by Penguin Books Australia Ltd 1998

1 3 5 7 9 10 8 6 4 2

Cover and text designed by Sandy Cull, Penguin Design Studio
Typeset in Bernhard Modern by Post Pre-press Group, Brisbane, Queensland
Printed and bound in Australia by Australian Print Group, Maryborough, Victoria

National Library of Australia
Cataloguing-in-Publication data:

Dowrick, Stephanie.
Daily acts of love.

ISBN 0 670 88393 X.

1. Love. 2. Forgiveness. 3. Virtues. I. Title.

179.9

Love that ends, is the

shadow of love.

True love is without

beginning or end.

HAZRAT INAYAT KHAN

We can all learn to express love
more openly and generously —
and so increase our own happiness as
well as the happiness of others.

Love lifts our spirits. It brings us
into connection with the best parts
of ourselves, and the finest aspects
of our shared humanity.

Most of us already know a great deal
about love. The lines in this small
book just bring some of that
into focus.

Compassion is the world's most perfect idea.
But it comes to life only when we practise it.

To be loving, you don't need to have someone special in your life.
The state of loving is special in itself.
It needs no particular goal.
No particular object.
It's a state of mind and heart.
A way of being.

Whatever it is that we pay most attention to will grow stronger in our lives.

Respect, delight, generosity,
forgiveness: these are
the essential foundations of love.
And humour is the canopy.

[4]

Should you doubt the force of life
and the power of renewal,
simply observe the miracle of a
blade of grass appearing through an
imperceptible crack in a mighty slab
of concrete.

Know the difference between love that asks for something, and love.

Look at the big picture.
Love is always there.

The primary meaning of the word love,
Buddhism teaches us, is friendship.
Honour friends as chosen family.
Honour family as you would your
dearest friends.

Love can be the rock of stability within your life, as well as the inspiration for it.

The deeper your knowledge of love, the more frequently you practise awareness of love, the greater your feeling of inner stability.

Unconditional love is a commitment
to go on loving *for love's sake*;
to go on appreciating the gift of life
for life's sake; to go on believing
there is good in humankind,
despite the failures, disappointments,
tragedies and mysteries that are
part of every human existence.

Treasure every person, living
creature or plant that reminds you
of what love is.

Love everything you do. Love it fiercely. Then more fiercely. Feel the transformation as you become part of your own ideas and actions and don't stand outside them.

A mantra of love can become the most exquisite comfort at times of stress.
Build up your knowledge of it through reciting it each day.
Allow it to become as familiar to you as breathing.
Rely on it as you would your breath.
There are many mantras. Here is just one:
Touching love, I breathe in.
Touching love, I breathe out.

Don't love your suffering and hurts only. Love your wildness, your creativity, your risk-taking, spontaneity, joy.
Love your optimism, determination, stubbornness.
Love the moment when everything is all right.

Discover how much more you hear
when you listen without judgement.

Isn't it wonderful to visit someone
who makes you abundantly welcome?
It is possible to be that welcoming
to all your friends and family: to
treat each one of them as an
honoured guest; to give as much care
to each visit as you would if you
knew this was to be the last.

Depend on friends.
But never take the gift of friendship
for granted.

Look to love for comfort.
Regard it as your refuge.
Return to your awareness of love
many times through each day.
Create reminders in all your
environments: REMEMBER
LOVE.

Love is the greatest of all cures — not least for loneliness.

Finding a cause or purpose beyond ourselves gives us a vital sense that life is worth living — whatever our personal circumstances, and whether or not we have someone to come home to.

To love someone else in their
entirety, we need to practise loving
all aspects of ourselves also.
We need to be able to see our faults,
acknowledge them, resist falling
into self-hatred, and skilfully
transform them.

Know who you are and where you came from.
Gather whatever positive memories you can of your family and ancestors.
Find out their stories of courage and survival.
Respect your heritage. Speak about it lovingly.

Read people's faces. See how
moving it is when love is expressed
in someone's features; when love
dances in their eyes. You can be
as beautiful as that.

Send love in all directions:
North, South, East, West.
Experience, for several dazzling
moments, how it is to be at the very
centre of the universe.

[23]

It is possible to move from infancy
to maturity in a single moment –
simply by acknowledging that other
people's feelings are as important
as your own.

Self-love cannot be developed
without also developing a dynamic,
committed concern for other
human beings.
Without that, it simply curdles
into narcissism.

Sometimes love requires us to stay in a difficult relationship and work at relieving those difficulties. But leaving a relationship that is debasing or dead is no less loving. The crucial point may not be whether we leave or stay, but how lovingly and respectfully we carry out our decision.

Blame no one when things
go wrong.
Ask only: 'What can I learn
from this?'

People can and often do
behave badly.
Is that any reason to avoid noticing
the thousand acts of kindness that
have also come your way?
Or to hold back from extending
a thousand acts of kindness
to others?

In the midst of even the worst crisis, it is possible to visualise a calm place within yourself. Give from that place. It will change what you are giving, and leave you far less depleted.

Know how large your circle
of compassion is.
Extend it daily.
Never exclude yourself.

Love soars when we don't overload it with demands.

Let your presence be a gift of love.

It is easy to mistake dependence
for love.
We *are* dependent on our intimate
relationships, but the more aware of
that we are, and the more willing we
are to be responsible for our own
happiness, the less tangled love and
dependency will be.

Step into the presence of just one
person who radiates love and you,
too, are positively affected.
Step into a moment of mindfulness
of love – think about bringing love
to the situation you are in – and you,
too, are positively affected.

Do some of the things you love
at half speed.
And then even more slowly.

Know what allows your spirit to dance.
Or have the finest time finding out.

Talk to yourself like a survivor —
not a victim.

It is easy to remember who has hurt you.
It is more challenging – and much more loving – to remember what you learned from surviving those hurts and moving on.

Self-love is most easily achieved
when you behave in ways that would
bear inspection.

Choose to do what is right.
Refuse to do what is wrong.
Each time you exercise your
knowledge of the difference between
right and wrong – between
benefiting or harming other human
beings – you grow in self-love, and
diminish self-defeat.

Do not remind yourself of people
or things that arouse negativity
or anger.
Remind yourself instead of what will
heal your pain, bring you contentment,
and strengthen you for the many
moments to come.

Give yourself a break from making judgements.
Occasionally just accept things as they are.

Try saying: 'I have enough.'
Then say: 'I have everything I need.'
Experience the relief!

Be aware of what you watch,
hear and read.
Does it nourish you?
Accept nothing less.

Sometimes we need grace to see what we can't change. And grace to see how that acceptance settles things within ourselves.

A baby smiles without judging
who is worthy of her smiles and who
is not.
We, too, can learn again to smile
without first judging.

Pleasing others can be wonderful. But not at the expense of your own self-respect and integrity.

No one loves a martyr. Not even
the martyr.
Do less. Love more.

Lie on clean white sheets.
Do nothing.

Love doesn't mean making excuses
to ourselves for behaving foolishly
or cruelly.
Love allows us to be tough enough
to live up to our highest standards.
To learn from our mistakes.
To do better.

Look long and hard at people who
live lovingly.
Notice how beautifully they age.
Notice how irrelevant their wealth
or status is.
Notice how much other people
want to be in their presence.
Notice how they smile.

Life is frequently unfair.
At such times, we should love more
fiercely. Not less.

What an incredible relief it is to discover that, in order to be happy, you don't always need to get what you most want.

Giving up self-righteousness for the sake of love is generally an excellent bargain.

No one can make you into a slave. When you must do something you would usually resent, choose the *attitude* you bring to the task. Choosing to do something wholeheartedly and well expresses your freedom. It also deepens your sense of honour and validates your self-respect.

Self-pity erodes love. When you feel sorry for yourself it is hard for others not to feel sorry for you at best, and irritated or contemptuous at worst. Guide others to view you positively.

Happiness is a state of mind, not
a destination. It is not necessary
to 'find love' before finding happiness.
Happiness arises from the way you
think about events: interpreting them
positively; finding what is good or
instructive; extending to
others the benefit of the doubt;
overlooking what is unimportant;
putting adversity behind you; setting
goals that are inspiring as well as
stimulating; cultivating your
creativity; engaging with life.

[57]

So much misery is a product of our
own thoughts.
Pay attention to what pleases you,
stimulates you or sustains you.
Discover – through experience – that
you can observe your thoughts.
And change them.

Kiss often.
Hug often.
Look into people's eyes.
Be glad.

It isn't easy to laugh and feel stressed at the same time.

Light many candles.

Take risks.
Fall in love with your own daring.

Sometimes tenderness is the only thing that will pierce the crust of our defences.

Tenderness is not sentimentality. Tenderness contains within it the seeds of acceptance that nothing within nature is entirely or eternally perfect. Nor is less moving for that.

Cultivate an attitude of tenderness
towards the parts of your face or
body you most dislike.
Look deeply into them, or at them.
See their fallibility, their transience,
their subtlety.

Is there any kind of rule that stops us from loving an imperfect body, loving it *because* it is imperfect and therefore human – and not despite its imperfections?

Love never sulks. Nor turns
its back.
Be familiar with how your body
feels when you are withdrawing love —
and how different it feels when you
are open to it.

There is nothing we can do to or through our bodies that does not affect the rest of who we are.

One of the most crucial ways to care for ourselves is through play. Children are happiest when their bodies feel free, and their hands are busy with clay, mud, sand, water, twigs, stones, shells, colour.
Adults are not so very different.

Eat something delicious with total enjoyment.
Love what you are doing. Love how good it tastes.
Pay close attention. Let the experience as well as the food fill you up.

Touch is one of the most profound
forms of communication.
Each time you touch someone, do it
with love.

Laughter and touch are the two forms of human communication that say more than language.

Offer touch that asks for nothing
in return.
Learn to massage the hands or feet
of the people you care for.
If someone you know is aged or ill,
or seldom touched, offer this gentle,
powerful massage, or simply to
wash their feet, or wash or brush
their hair.

Before we begin to grasp the unity of all things, we live in a dream.

Find time for making love, not just for having sex.

If sex no longer feels like the giving and receiving of love, a change of view is needed.

Or a decision to move on.

Love transforms sex. Deepens it,
and then deepens it some more.
Love makes sex matter more — and
less. It encourages laughter,
play, utter foolishness.
It teaches tenderness. Respect. Awe.
Love makes passion last. Forever.

We see someone at their most perfect when we first fall in love. Psychology teaches us that we must then learn to accept all their imperfections. And this is true. But shouldn't we also remember their perfection?
This is also true.

Passion is not something we feel only when we are young. Nor do we feel it only for another person. Passion is an attitude that is ageless, energising, transforming.

When we do something passionately, we are living right in the present moment. It's the best kind of active meditation because, in that moment, we are also alive to what is universal and eternal.

Never take love for granted.
Cultivate an attitude of deep respect
for the people you love, and
gratitude for their presence in
your life.
Express this in every way
you can.

Love is not possessive.
Possessiveness arises from fear, not
love. It speaks of a misplaced belief
that we can make ourselves safe by
owning or controlling another person.
Love allows us to feel safe and whole
within ourselves. This leaves us free
to reach out without grasping –
and to rediscover trust.

Things you would never do for money are often amazingly easy to do for love.

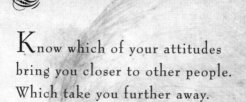

Know which of your attitudes
bring you closer to other people.
Which take you further away.

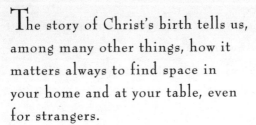

The story of Christ's birth tells us,
among many other things, how it
matters always to find space in
your home and at your table, even
for strangers.
The space must first be found,
however, in your heart.

Often what is most loving is
also most practical.
Before enlightenment: feed people,
wash dishes.
After enlightenment: feed people,
wash dishes.

Recognise who people are – beyond their usefulness.

Human love is the best expression
we have of divine love.
But essential to human love is
accepting that our beloved
is not divine.

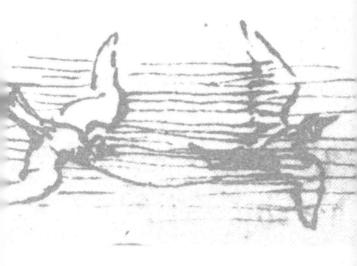

It is possible to take the sting out of
envy when you learn to be pleased
for someone else, to be delighted for
their sake.

You have a huge amount of power
to encourage others.
Use it.

There is a unique joy in overcoming
your distaste for a particular
activity in order to ease the life
of someone else.

You are fed up with your partner's habit of calling out to ask if you're thinking of putting on some coffee. You are ready to shout, 'Put it on yourself!' Instead, not only do you make coffee, you put the pot and mug on a tray, with a plate of biscuits and flowers in a vase. Not because you have to. Not because you must. But only because you are *free to do so*.

Emotional intelligence is part
of love.
It arises first from self-awareness:
a willingness to be clear about the
effect you have on others, and a
willingness to make instant changes
when those effects are anything
but positive.

Know exactly what it means to project your unwanted negative feelings onto other people. Refusing to make other people 'bad' because you feel bad builds maturity, and lasting power.

The rule of thumb on human behaviour is so simple. Doing what harms others will hurt you also. Doing what relieves others or offers them happiness will at least bring you peace.

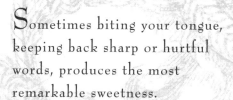

Sometimes biting your tongue, keeping back sharp or hurtful words, produces the most remarkable sweetness.

When people work together to find
a solution to a painful difference, their
connection is markedly deepened.
Welcome those trying patches as an
opportunity to support your decision
to be together.

Love cannot be forced.
In trying to force something or
someone in the name of love, we
are confusing love with ego.
Let your knowledge of love soften
the demands of ego.

You can't look at someone and hurry past them at the same time.

Honour your obligations. They are a privilege of your relationships.

It can be immensely loving to resist
the temptation to point out someone
else's faults or failings.
We find it easy enough to overlook
our own. Extend that kindness
to others.

Love thrives in the presence of commitment.

No matter how gorgeous the things you give are, they aren't substitutes for truthfulness, constancy, respect, time, laughter, care.

If you are neglecting the rest of your life in order to make money for your family, it is good to ask them, 'Do you want this?'

Know what lifts the spirits of the people you love.
Don't stint on that.

Give those you love all the space and solitude they need.
Use that time as an opportunity to discover more about your own inner life, or to deepen your connections with other friends.

*T*hank *you* is a great way to say
I love you.

If you have difficulty with the magic words *I love you*, fix it.

What expressions of love do you want most for yourself?
That may be the best place to begin when considering how to express love to others.

If you are tempted to criticise someone, praise them instead. The rewards will astonish you.

Other people can affect your happiness, but they are not responsible for it.
Love *gives* happiness. It does not demand it.

Add something beautiful to the table at every meal, especially when it is 'just' family, or, most of all, when it is 'just' you.

Discover what you can afford
to overlook.

Appreciation wonderfully expresses
love.

Bring a wide range of interests to
the people you love.
Extend your conversations
beyond your own immediate,
familiar experiences.
Think about the people you would
most like to have dinner with.
Imagine how stimulating their
talk would be. How carefully they
would listen.
Copy them.

Allow an acquaintance to become
a friend, a friend to become a lover,
a hobby to become a passion, a wish
to become a reality.
A treasured life is replete with risks,
adventures, experiences.

Grow flowers.
Buy flowers.
Cherish their variety.

Is there something beautiful in every room you live or work in?

Practise giving anonymously.
There is real freedom in giving
without expectation of praise
or thanks.

Any act of selfless giving expands
your world outwards.

Whatever our differences, we share this: we want to love, and we want to be loved.
What separates us is the way we go about it.

We rarely know what is best for someone else without asking them.

Love is not a commodity. You debase it when you use it to coerce or threaten another human being. You also debase yourself.
Love allows you to pull back from such behaviour; to look deeply into the eyes of that person and recover your wish never to hurt them.

It is not possible to claim to love
someone and also treat them as
the rubbish bin for your anger
and frustration.
If you truly love that person, deal
with your frustrations elsewhere.
If you do not love them,
let them go.

When the impulse arises to attack
someone, work it out physically.
Go for a run or a swim.
Get into a room by yourself and yell.
Beat cushions.
Get to a gym and cycle until your
legs shriek.
Later, ask yourself why that person
had the power to upset you so much.
Later still, and only when you are
calm, talk about it.

When someone begins to
attack you, walk away.
Only when that person is calm,
listen to what they have to say.

As long as we judge people as being
more or less worthy of love, we are
confusing the value of their life
with the value of their actions.
We can love some actions more,
and some less.
We can admire some behaviours,
despise others.
But love asks more of us than that.
No matter how foul someone's life
is, how devastating their actions,
that person remains as deserving
of love as you or I.

[124]

Someone who is mean-spirited, boastful, deceitful, angry or attacking is expressing a lack of love and poor self-regard, however 'puffed up' they may outwardly appear.

This doesn't mean that you should condone their actions. But it may allow you to regard the person with more compassion.

Betrayal can be as connective
as love.
The person you want to think of
least may become the person you
think of constantly.
The first step in forgiveness can be
taken for your sake only: to loosen
your connections to the past.
To bring you into the present
moment.

Sometimes it is possible only to love someone's soul.
Or just to ask God or the universe to do the loving for you.
Don't underestimate how that small step can begin to free you from the misery of wishing harm to someone else.

In thinking about love, it is useful to be able to distinguish between a slight and a hurt; between a disappointment and a tragedy; between the need for something to be excused, and the need for someone to be forgiven.

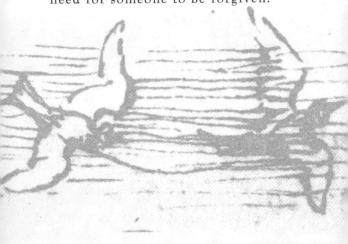

Compassion arises when you think less about your difficulties with forgiveness and more about the insights your suffering has brought you.

Forgiveness does not condone
what is wrong.
It simply says: whatever you have
done, you are still a member of the
human family.
Whatever you have done, I refuse
to wish you harm.
Whatever you have done, I have
the power to retrieve wisdom and
compassion from my own suffering.

Looking around us, we can see
that others also suffer.
And that we can help.
We can see that the seasons of
suffering are often and quite
incredibly followed by seasons
of joy, wisdom, insight.
And that we can help.
We can see that the suffering is
sometimes of our own making.
And that we can help.

Apologise when someone is hurt
by an action of yours – *even when
you did not mean to hurt them or do
not think that what you have
done is wrong.*
'I am sorry my action or words
caused you pain. I regret that.'

Other lives matter.
Imagine the world we would live
in if we could put that simple truth
into action.

The moment we leave our comfort zone in order to help someone else, or to ally ourselves with a cause greater than ourselves, we risk becoming a bigger person.

The most emotionally healthy people in our society are able to put themselves into other people's shoes, know how someone else is feeling, and care about that.

This capacity extends beyond sexual and family intimacy. It creates a circle of genuine feeling that can extend, eventually, to all of humankind.

We can be part of the world's brutality. Or we can choose to do whatever we can to relieve it.

Luck is a hugely underestimated factor in anyone's circumstances. See others' misfortunes as a failure of luck. See it as your good luck to be able to help.

[137]

Tolerance expresses a commitment
to the belief that none of us has
a life more precious than another's.
This idea is so challenging to our
judgemental mind that we can
come towards an understanding of it
only through the experience of
universal love.
'I may not like what you stand for.
I may hate almost everything you do
and say. Yet I still will not deny that
you, too, are a member of the
human family.'

Each time we choose to make
a positive difference to one person's
life, we become part of the vital
flow of good.
Each time we refuse to make such
a difference, we impede that flow.

Poverty is a violence that affects
all our lives – but not equally.
Love allows us to give most to those
who suffer most.

Violence and war will never end until we listen to those who have suffered.

In every situation you are in, be aware of who feels most left out. Take that opportunity to bring someone more closely into the heart of the human family.

Accommodating ourselves to other people's needs, we create community.

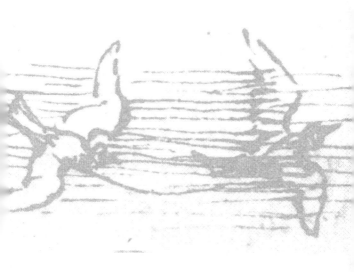

We are all walking in each other's
footsteps, standing on each other's
shoulders, learning from each
other's brilliance, and suffering
from each other's griefs.
It is sobering and comforting to
reflect on how inevitably we are
a part of a single human family.

How can you best serve humanity?
Finding answers to this question
brings meaning to your life.

Sometimes it is easier to serve humanity than it is to be good tempered at the breakfast table. Never treat those closest to you with any less respect than you would the highest causes with which you are associated.

It may not be possible even to glimpse true happiness while others suffer.
It certainly is not possible to feel true happiness when you cause others to suffer.

The mother gazes at her baby
with the eyes of love – and finds
perfection.
We can learn to see all living
creatures with that same gaze.
Ourselves, also.

The richest people in our society
are those who can give without
feeling in any way diminished
by giving.
This has nothing to do with money.
It has everything to do with feelings
of self-love and abundance.

When you are faced with a difficult
decision, ask yourself, 'Which
outcome would be more loving?'
A loving outcome is not based on
fear or greed, or the ego's desire to
be placated.
A loving outcome acknowledges
reality, respects everyone involved,
and speaks the truth.

Never underestimate how powerfully nature herself can support us. When you feel low, leave your home, throw yourself into moving water; walk vigorously on grass, earth or sand; touch shells; watch the moon rise or the sun set; count stars; feel the wind or rain sting your face. Recognise that nature is simultaneously chaotic, indifferent and exquisitely well ordered. Relish being part of that.

The quality of our relationships
is not determined by age, colour,
wealth, gender or sexuality.
The quality of our relationships
is determined only by our
consciousness of love.

Love is always present.
It is we who forget it – or remember.

STEPHANIE DOWRICK is the author of a number of much-loved international bestsellers, including *Forgiveness and Other Acts of Love*, *Intimacy and Solitude*, *The Intimacy and Solitude Self-Therapy Book* and two novels, *Running Backwards Over Sand* and *Tasting Salt*. She is the mother of two teenagers, and a regular contributor to radio and newspapers.